Index of Projects

Fabulous Fob Ornament
pages 11 - 13

Herringbone Bracelet
pages 14 - 18

Pillow Bead Key Chain
pages 19 - 24

Long Beaded Necklace
pages 25 - 30

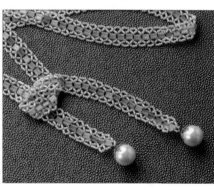

Netted Lariat Necklace
pages 31 - 33

Tila Link Bracelet
pages 34 - 36

Shaped Herringbone Pendant
pages 37 - 43

Figures of 8 Necklace
pages 44 - 48

Wave Bracelet
pages 49 - 51

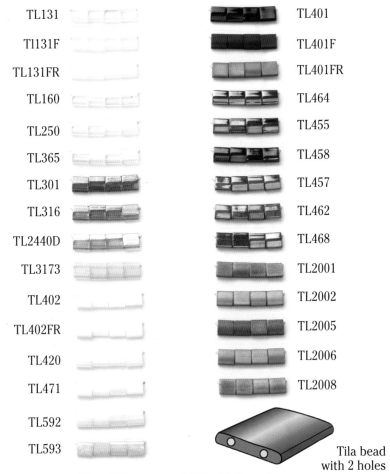

TL131	TL401
Tl131F	TL401F
TL131FR	TL401FR
TL160	TL464
TL250	TL455
TL365	TL458
TL301	TL457
TL316	TL462
TL2440D	TL468
TL3173	TL2001
TL402	TL2002
TL402FR	TL2005
TL420	TL2006
TL471	TL2008
TL592	
TL593	

Tila bead
with 2 holes

The History of Tila™ Beads

TILA beads (pronounced tie-la or tee-la) are wonderful beads from MIYUKI Co., Ltd. Well known as the inventor of Delica cylinder beads, MIYUKI's latest innovation is a flat, 2-hole, 5mm square bead made from a unique process that creates a silky smooth surface and a beautifully uniform shape.

MIYUKI puts its spirit into every TILA square. TILA beads measure 5x5x1.9mm. One side of the TILA has little weave on the surface so beads threaded in a sheet are attractive to the touch, and with 31 colors, pleasing to the eye as well. TILA beads work well with traditional peyote, herringbone, and other square stitches.

Alice Korach

Alice Korach is the founding editor of Bead&Button Magazine. Her idea was that there were many people like her who want to know how to create beautiful beadwork.

Alice took up beading when she was eight and knitting at eleven. She has always loved teaching and sharing her skills and knowledge with others. Alice has always known that she is a good technician and a skilled designer. Practicing art in three-dimensional glass sculptures freed her to an artistic flowering in other forms of bead art as well.

Alice teaches at national conventions and shops, particularly at the 'Bead Needs' shop in Hales Corners, Wisconsin.

www.LostWaxGlass.com
Alice Korach
518 McCall St.,
Waukesha, WI 53186

Needles

The large holes in all Delica sizes make it possible to work many of these projects with size 10 beading needles.

However, you will have to use size 12 or 13 needles for projects that incorporate seed beads or have many thread passes.

Threads

You should, of course, use your favorite needles and threads. Many beaders swear by the strength of Fireline, but I haven't used it since a piece I'd woven on Fireline came apart in a million pieces. I was a Nymo beader until very recently Kobayashi introduced the same new nylon filament thread in slightly different palettes. Kobayashi's new thread is K-O. The weight is similar to Nymo B, but the thread has a slick coating that causes it to resist fraying without needing any type of thread conditioner (beeswax or Thread Heaven). It also seems to be comparable in strength to Nymo D. K-O has recently produced a D weight that seems much stronger than Nymo D.

K-O and Nymo both need to be prestretched before you begin to weave. K-O is very stretchy, so prestretching will prevent your beadwork from becoming loose over time. It also uncoils the thread, which helps minimize tangling. As with any thread, you should thread the needle with the end that comes off the spool first so you are sewing with the thread's grain to minimize fraying.

If you are using beads with sharp edges, such as crystals or some cuts, you may prefer to use Fireline or Power Pro (BeadCats sells a generic version of the latter at a much reduced price). I used K-O for all the projects in this book.

Scissors and Glue

My favorite beading scissors are high-quality, Solingen steel manicure scissors. They're very sharp, sturdy, and come to a tiny point. Good-quality "stork" embroidery scissors also work well. When cutting off thread tails, use a trick Virginia Blakelock teaches and pull on the thread as you cut it. This stretches it slightly so the end hides inside the last bead. Never cut a thread immediately after a knot; pass it through a few beads before cutting, or the knot will come untied.

If you use clear nail polish as glue for your knots, apply a drop from the tip of your beading needle directly on the knot (another Virginia Blakelock trick). Never use the nail polish brush; the solvent could damage bead color or finish. I recommend G-S Hypo Cement for knots at the end of pearl strands.

Surgeon's Knot

The surgeon's knot starts like a square knot.

1. Cross the left-hand end on top of the right-hand end, wrap it behind the right-hand cord, and bring it back to the front (lower blue line). The right-hand tail (red) now points left and the left-hand tail points right.

2. Bend the right-hand tail (red) back toward the right and the left-hand tail back toward the left (middle of knot).

3. Cross the tail that's currently on the right (blue), over the tail coming from the left (red).

4. Wrap it behind that tail and pull it through the opening between the step 1 cross and the step 3 cross (this is a square knot).

5. To turn it into a surgeon's knot wrap behind, under, and through to the front again. The result is that the top of the knot curves partway down the sides of the first cross, which makes it more stable and unlikely to twist out of the square when you tighten it.

6. Pull the tails in the directions they are pointing to tighten knot.

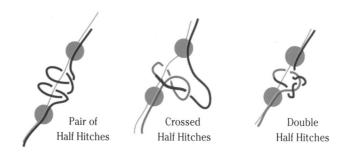

Pair of Half Hitches   Crossed Half Hitches   Double Half Hitches

Half-Hitch Knot

1. For a plain half hitch, bring the needle through a bead. Then sew under the thread between this bead and the next bead. Tighten until a small loop remains.

2. Pass the needle through the loop, going over the thread that you previously sewed under (lower loop in pair of half hitches).

3. Repeat the process for a paired half hitch, which is more secure than a single half hitch.

4. For a crossed half hitch, repeat step 1 of the plain half hitch. Give the starting loop a half twist so its sides cross (red loop on right), then sew through it. Tighten carefully so it doesn't lock too soon.

5. Start a double half hitch like a plain half hitch, but sew through the loop twice. This knot is prone to tightening prematurely.

Crimping

You can press a crimp flat with chain-nose pliers, but crimping pliers fold the crimp so it is less visible and slightly more secure. The jaws of crimping pliers have two stations. The one closer to the handles looks like a crescent moon, and the one at the end of the pliers is oval.

1. Separate the wires in the crimp with one hand and place the crimp in the crescent moon station of the pliers. Press firmly. The goal is to have one wire on each side of the dent that this station puts into the crimp.

2. Turn the dented crimp sideways so the dent is centered between the pliers jaws in the oval station.

3. Press down smoothly to fold the crimp at the dent. For security, you may want to press the fold together with chain-nose pliers.

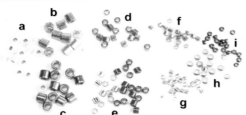

Bead	size	type	width (mm)	length (mm)
Delica	8/0	cut	3.0	3.0
Delica	8/0	plain	3.0	3.0
Round	8/0		3.0	2.0
Delica	10/0	cut	2.2	1.7
Delica	10/0	plain	2.2	1.7
Round	11/0		2.0	1.4
Delica	11/0	cut	1.6	1.4
Delica	11/0	plain	1.6	1.4
Round	15/0		1.5	1.0

Delica beads, also known generically as Japanese cylinder beads, are cylindrical in shape and very regular. They were invented by Mr. Masayoshi Katsuoka, president of Miyuki Company, in the early 1980s, and the original size, 11/0, arrived in the United States in 1987. Size 8/0 followed in the mid-1990s. And Miyuki developed the new size 10/0 within the last year.

All three sizes come in both the original plain cylinder and the hexagonal or "cut" shape. You will find very few irregular beads in packages of size 10 and 11 plain Delicas. Size 8/0 Delicas evince slightly more irregularity; and while cuts have been fire polished to produce smooth edges, a few may have sharp ends, so choose them with care.

In fact, to get the best results, you should always select Delicas and other kinds of beads carefully; even in the most regular of brands there will always be slight size and length variations in a package.

Seed beads are measured across the width of their hole (the diameter) to determine size. The length of the hole is irrelevant to their size; although it has a major impact on what kinds of beads can be used together. Using different length beads together, however, can create remarkable texture.

The type of finish applied to the bead may also affect its size slightly. Even glass type has an effect on size – black beads of any type are almost always a bit smaller than other colors of the same type for example.

In the photo, beads a, b, and c at left are all size 8/0. Notice the two a and b beads that are aligned hole to hole in the photo. While their width is almost identical, the difference in their length is dramatic. Size 8/0 round seed beads (a) average about 2.9mm in width but are about 2mm in length. Cut (b) and plain (c) size 8/0 Delicas average 2.9 to 3.05mm in width but are almost 1mm longer than round size 8/0s.

Beads d & e are size 10/0 Delicas; the d beads are cuts & the e beads are plain. Cut size 10/0 Delicas average 2.05mm in width & 1.65mm in length. Plain size 10/0 Delicas are a hair narrower & longer. Size 10/0 Delicas are closest in size to size 11/0 round Japanese seed beads (h), which average 2.15mm in width but are about 0.3mm shorter. The similarity in size of 10/0 Delicas & 11/0 Miyuki seeds makes them suitable to be used together.

Size 11/0 Delicas (f cuts & g) are markedly smaller than size 11/0 seed beads (h) but only a little larger than size 15/0 seed beads (i), revealed by the adjacent f & i beads lying on their sides. Delica size 11/0 beads (f & g) average 1.7mm in width & 1.4mm in length. Size 15/0 round seed beads (i) vary a lot in any given package but average 1.6mm in width & 1mm in length.

Dutch Spiral Adjustable Necklace

Wear this necklace either as a choker or a neckline length.

The fancy Dutch spiral front section makes it a standout.

Dutch Spiral Adjustable Necklace

continued from page 7

SIZE: 15"

Materials - Dark Charcoal Necklace

109 Tila beads, matte metallic dark gray AB (T)
3-5g Triangle beads, Size 8/0, black-lined crystal (B)
2-3g Triangle beads, Size 10/0, gold-lined crystal luster (G)
7g Delica Beads, size 10/0 sparkle flesh-lined crystal (D)
5g Seed beads, size 8/0, dark bronze (8/0)
2 Czech pressed-glass cathedral beads, sapphire and Picasso
2 Czech pressed-glass oval window beads, sapphire with purple luster
36" (.9m) Flexible beading wire, size .010
2 Clam-shell bead tips, antique bronze
2 Crimp beads, size 1 x 1mm or micro crimps
1 Spring ring clasp, antique bronze, 10mm
2" (5cm) Long-and-short chain, antique bronze
1 Teardrop charm, antique bronze, 10mm long
1 Oval jump ring, antique bronze. 5 x 4mm
2 Oval jump rings, antique bronze, 4 x 3mm
Beading thread, K-O black or dark red
Beading needles, size 12
Bead stopper or alligator clip

Materials - Light Pearlized Necklace

109 Tila beads, white AB (T)
3-5g Triangle beads, Size 8/0, white crystal (B)
2-3g Triangle beads, Size 10/0, silver-lined crystal luster (G)
7g Delica Beads, size 10/0 sparkle white crystal (D)
5g Seed beads, size 8/0, irridescent pink (8/0)
2 Czech pressed-glass cathedral beads, crystal AB
2 Czech pressed-glass oval window beads, crystal AB
36" (.9m) Flexible beading wire, size .010
2 Clam-shell bead tips, gold
2 Crimp beads, size 1 x 1mm or micro crimps
1 Spring ring clasp, gold, 10mm
2" (5cm) Long-and-short chain, gold
1 Teardrop charm, gold, 10mm long
1 Oval jump ring, gold. 5 x 4mm
2 Oval jump rings, gold, 4 x 3mm
Beading thread, K-O white
Beading needles, size 12
Bead stopper or alligator clip

How-to

See Materials for bead color abbreviations.

First Half of the Strung Necklace

1. Cut the flexible beading wire into two equal lengths. Crimp one end of the two pieces together tightly. String the long wires out a bead tip with the crimp inside

Close the bead tip. Press the two halves of each clamshell together to close the bead tips and roll the handle into a neat round loop. (Hint: for best security, roll the handle into a loop before closing the clam shell with the tip of the handle just below the top of the shell.

Put a drop of glue into the shell and close it with pliers so that the tip of the handle is inside the shell. Hold the pliers in place for a minute or two until the glue has begun to set – photos 1 & 2.)

2. Over both wires, string a B, an 8/0, and a G.

3. Separate the wires and on each, string D, B, D, 8/0, and a Tila, one wire through each hole.

4. Now string the following pattern 5 times on the separated wires: 8/0, D, B, D, 8/0, and a Tila.

After stringing the 6th Tila, finish the first half of the bead strand as follows:

   a. With the wires separated, string 8/0, D, B, and D.

   b. Hold the wires together as one and string G, 8/0, B, then a window bead. String B, 8/0, G then a cathedral bead.

5. Continue holding the two wires together and string about 5" (12.7cm) of Ds around which you'll form the Dutch spiral. Clamp them off so the necklace is firm with a Bead Stopper or an alligator clip.

Dutch Spiral Center

1. Start by stringing an 8/0, a D, a G, a B, and a T. Tie the tail to the working thread to form a firm ring of beads around the string of Ds on the doubled wire (figure 1, a-b), using a Surgeon's knot (see "Knots" on page 5).

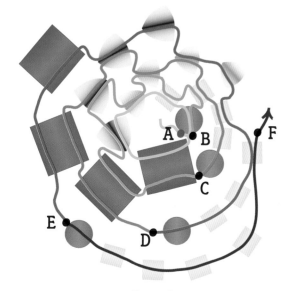

Figure 1

2. With the needle exiting the T, continue through the 8/0. Pick up a D and go through the D on the ring. *Pick up a G and go through the G on the ring. Pick up a B and go through the B on the ring. Pick up a T and go through the free hole on the previous T* (figure 1, b-c).

3. For the third round, pick up an 8/0 and 2D. Go through the D on the previous round. Repeat *-* of step 2 (figure 1, c-d).

4. Begin round 4 with an 8/0 and 3D. Go through the 2nd D (the last) of round 3. Repeat *-* of step 2 (figure 1, d-e). Note: every round will end this way.

5. Begin round 5 with an 8/0 and 4D. Go through the last D of round 4 (figure 1, e-f) and end *-*.

6. Work round 6 like round 5, but pick up 5D. On round 7, pick up 6D, and on round 8, pick up 7D.

7. On the next 6 rounds, pick up 6, 5, 4, 3, 2, then 1D, working the rest of each round as normal.

8. For the next 6 rounds, pick up 2, 3, 4, 5, 6, then 7D, working the rest of each round as normal.

Dutch Spiral Adjustable Necklace
continued from page 9

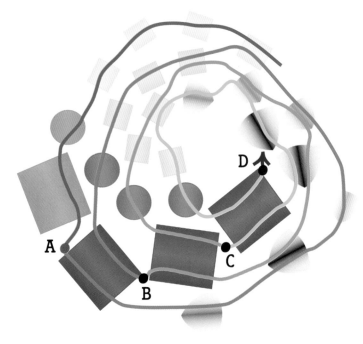

Figure 2

9. Alternate steps 7 and 8, ending with a 4D length in step 7. This group attaches to the second hole of the fourth-to-last Tila (figure 2, a).

10. To complete the spiral:

a. Pick up the third-to-last T and go through the previous B. Pick up a B and go through the last G. Pick up a G and go through the nearest D. Pick up 3D and an 8/0. Go through the second hole of the new Tila (figure 2, a-b).

b. Pick up a Tila, go through the last B, pick up a B and go through the last G. Pick up a G and go through the third D from the last 8/0 added. Pick up 2D and an 8/0 and go through the last Tila (figure 2, b-c).

c. Pick up the last Tila, and go through the previous B and add a B. Go through the previous G and add a G. Go through the second D from the last 8/0. Pick up a D and an 8/0. Then go through the second hole of the last Tila (figure 2, c-d). Go through the second hole of the Tila and end the beadwork with 2-3 pairs of half hitches between beads before trimming it.

Remainder of Strung Necklace

1. Add or remove Ds to completely fill the Dutch spiral. They shouldn't show on the ends of the spiral.

2. Repeat the stringing pattern on the wires in reverse from steps 4b through 2.

3. Pass both wire tails inside the other bead tip. Make sure there are no gaps between beads on the necklace length and string a crimp over the pair of wire tails snug against the inner bottom of the bead tip. Crimp it tightly then trim off the excess wire and close the bead tip.

Clasp Finishing

1. Use a small jump ring to attach the spring ring to the loop on one of the bead tips.

2. Cut the chain so it is about 2" (5cm) long and begins and ends with a short link. Use the other small jump ring to attach one end of the chain to the other bead tip loop.

3. Use the larger jump ring to attach the teardrop dangle to the end link on the chain.

Fabulous Fob Ornament

Plain bronze-colored rings become something special when jacketed in Tila beads, seed beads, and faceted glass beads.

See Materials for bead color abbreviations.

SIZE: 1⅛" x 2"

Materials

17 Tila beads, metallic bright green (T)
1 Antique-look bronze ring, ID14mm, OD 21mm
1 Antique-look bronze ring, ID18.5mm, OD 26.5mm
2 Twist-look antique bronze jump rings, 7mm
Dangle hardware
1 Backed crystal rhinestone, 4 holes, 6 x 4mm
12 Czech faceted pressed-glass beads, 4mm, dark bronze
1-2g Seed beads, size 11/0, dark bronze
Beading thread, green K-O or transparent
Beading needles, size 12

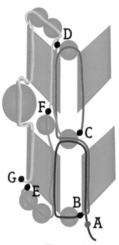

Figure 1

Small Ring

Start on the inside edge of the first bead wrap.

1. Leaving a 4-6" (10-15cm) thread tail, string 1 T, a seed bead, a T, and a seed bead (figure 1, a-b). Continue through the same hole of the first T and the first seed.

2. String a T, a seed, and a T (figure 1, b-c). Continue through the seed you exited at the end of step 1 and the first T added in this step (figure 1, c-d).

3. String 2 seeds and go down the other hole of the same T. String a pressed glass bead and go through the second hole of the T below (figure 1, d-e).

4. String 2 seeds and go up the first hole of the same T. String 1 seed (figure 1, e-f). Go up the first hole of the T above.

5. Continue through the 2 seeds above the top T. Then sew down to the bottom through the top T, the pressed-glass bead, and the bottom T (figure 1, f-g).

6. To begin the front of the wrap, string 2 seeds and place the beadwork on the small ring with the seeds you just strung about ⅛" (3mm) before a hole in the ring. The pressed-glass bead should be against the outer edge of the ring.

Fabulous Fob Ornament

continued from page 11

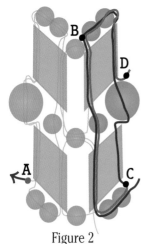

Figure 2

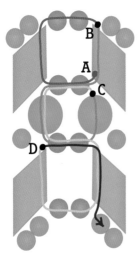

Figure 3

7. Sew up the first hole of the first T strung. Pick up a seed and sew up the hole above on the other T (figure 2, a-b).

8. Pick up 2 seeds, sew down the outside edge hole of the same T and string the second pressed-glass bead.

9. Sew down the outside hole of the first T (figure 2, b-c).

10. Go through the 2 seeds added in step 6. Continue up the inside hole on the first T, the single seed, and the inside hole of the second T. Go through the 2 seeds added in step 8 and down the outside hole of the top T (figure 2, c-d).

11. To finish the outside edge, pick up 2 seeds and sew up the outside hole on the other top T. Pick up 2 seeds (figure 3, a-b). Go down the outside hole of the first top T and through the first pair of seeds added in this step.

12. Sew down the first pressed-glass bead, pick up 2 seeds, and sew up the second pressed-glass bead (figure 3, b-c).

13. Circle through the same 2 seeds at the beginning of step 12, the first pressed-glass bead, and the 2 seeds added at the end of step 12.

14. Sew down the outside edge of the first T, pick up 2 seeds, and sew up the outside edge of the other T (figure 3, c-d).

Continue through 2 seeds below 2 pressed-glass beads and go down the first T. End the working thread and starting tail with a few pairs of half-hitches between beads.

15. Repeat steps 1-14 on the other side of the bottom hole on the ring with its bottom edge

beads 1/8" (3mm) away from the hole. There will be about a 1/4" (6mm) space between the two jackets with a hole in the middle of it.

16. Use a twist-look jump ring to attach the dangle hardware to the top hole on the ring.

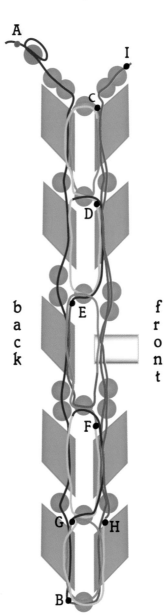

Figure 4

Large Ring

Start the bead wrap for the large ring at the top inside edge.

1. String a stop bead 4-6" (10-15cm) from the end of the thread. Pick up 2 seeds, a T, 1 seed, a T, 2 seeds, a T, 2 seeds, a T, 1 seed, and a T (figure 4, a-b).

The seeds will lie against the inner edge of the ring's center hole with the Ts against the back side of the ring, but don't work on the ring until instructed to do so.

2. In this step, you add the beads for the front of the ring joining them to the previous beads only at the top and the bottom:

Pick up a seed, a T, a seed, and a T. Pick up 2 seeds and string through the shorter hole on the rhinestone gem (it will align vertically at the center of the ring).

Pick up 2 seeds, a T, 1 seed, and a T (figure 4, b-c).

3. Now join the front and back beads at the inner edge fold. Pick up 1 seed and go down the hole you went through on the first T (step 1).

Pick up a seed. Circle through the inner edge hole of the front end T, the first seed you added in this step, the adjacent hole on the back T, and the second seed added in this step (figure 4, c-d).

4. Continue down the next T on the front side, Pick up 1 seed and go up the near hole on the back side T.

Continue through the last seed you went through in step 4, the front T of this step, and the seed added in this step (figure 4, d-e).

5. Go through the third back T. Pick up 1 seed, and go up the inner edge hole on the gem then the seed you added in the previous step.

Continue through the third back T and the seed you added in this step (figure 4, e-f).

6. Go through the third front T, pick up a seed, and sew up the fourth back T.

Continue through the seed you added in the previous step, the third front T and the seed added in this step (figure 4, f-g).

7. Go down the fifth back T then through the bottom seed you picked up at the beginning of step 4. Sew up the fourth front T and go through the seed added in the previous step.

Continue to circle through the fifth back T, the bottom seed, and the fourth front T (figure 4, g-h).

8. Sew up the same holes of the beads added in step 2 and string 2 seeds (figure 4, h-i).

9. Now you add beads between the front side Ts as follows:
Sew down the other hole of the top T, string a pressed-glass bead, go through the next T, string a pressed-glass bead and a seed.

 Go through the other hole on the gem. String a seed and a pressed-glass bead. Go through the third T, string a pressed-glass bead and go through the fourth T and pick up 2 seeds (figure 5, a-b).

10. Sew up the inner edge hole of the same T and circle through the inside fold seed then down the bottom back T.

Pick up 2 seeds and sew up the outside edge hole of the bottom back T (figure 5, b-c).

11. Add beads between the outside edge holes of the back Ts as follows:

String a pressed-glass bead, go through the next T, string a pressed-glass bead and a seed and go through the third T. String a seed and a pressed glass bead, go through the fourth T. String a pressed-glass bead, and go through the fifth T.

Remove the stop bead and sew through the first 2 seeds added in the first step (figure 5, c-d).

12. To position your needle to join the front and back, go down the inside edge hole of the first back T, through the seed between it and the adjacent front T (figure 5, d-e).

Sew up the inner edge hole of the front T, through the two beads along its outside edge and down the other hole on the front T (figure 5, e-f).

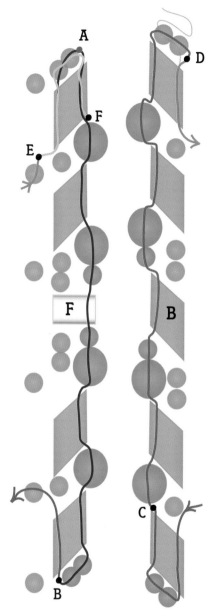

Figure 5

Fabulous Fob Ornament

continued from page 13

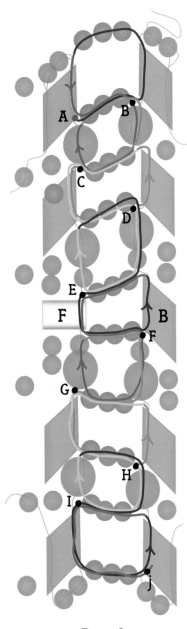

Figure 6

Closing the Beadwork on the Large Ring

Place the beads on the large ring with the back beads on the back, the single seeds against the inner edge of the center hole, and the front beads against the front.

Center the gem over one of the holes in the ring. Work circles of beads connecting the front and back Ts as described:

1. String 3 seeds and sew up the outside edge hole of the back T. String 3 seeds, go down the same hole on the front T, and continue through the first 3 seeds strung in this step (figure 6, a-b).

2. Sew down the back pressed-glass bead, pick up 3 seeds, and sew up the front pressed-glass bead. Circle through the 3 seeds before the pressed-glass beads, the back pressed-glass bead and the 3 seeds added in this step (figure 6, b-c).

3. Make another 3-seed circle between the second pair of Ts, adding 3 seeds below them and ending by coming through the newest group of 3 seeds (figure 6, c-d).

4. Repeat step 2 but remember that the pressed-glass beads consist of a pressed-glass and a seed bead (figure 6, d-e).

5. Make another 3-seed circle between the third back T and the gem, ending by coming through the newest group of 3 seeds (figure 6, e-f).

6. Repeat step 4 (figure 6, f-g) then 3 (figure 6, g-h), 2 (figure 6, h-i), and 1 (figure 6, i-j). End both the working thread and the starting tail with several pairs of half-hitches between beads.

7. Use the other twist-look jump ring to join the free top hole of the large ring to the bottom hole between the bead jackets on the small ring.

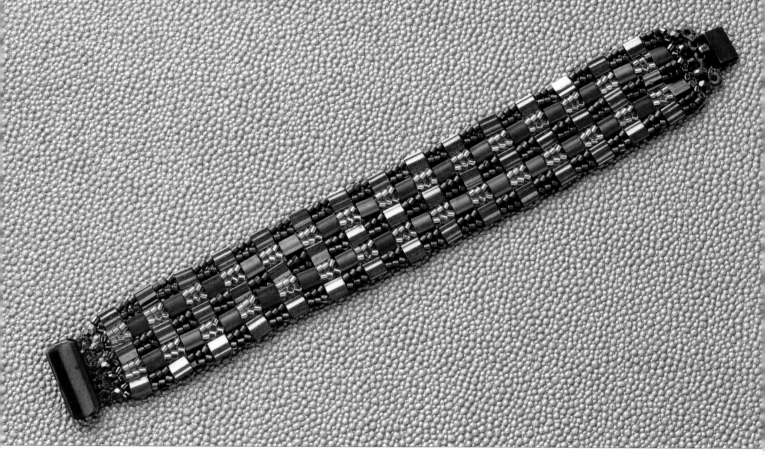

Herringbone Bracelet

This bracelet will look best if you choose two colors of Delica beads that have a similar tone because thread will show on the outside of some of them, so one thread color will blend with both.

SIZE: 7"

Materials

2 Colors of Tila beads, approx.:
- 45 metallic bright bronze (A)
- 30 matte metallic bronze luster (B)

3 colors size 10/0 Delica beads:
- 6-7g matte metallic bronze luster (MC)
- 5g gold-lined clear (AC)
- 1g dark bronze

10 Czech faceted pressed glass beads, 3mm, dark bronze

Beading thread, K-O, tan or brown

Beading needles, size 10 or 12

1 Box clasp, antique bronze, 5-loop, 20mm long

Preparing the Clasp

Before beginning to bead, use doubled beading thread to work a tight buttonhole stitch around the outside of all the loops on each clasp part as shown in the detail photo above.

Herringbone Bracelet

continued from page 15

1. Work the first 5-6 buttonhole stitches over the thread tail to anchor it securely, after which you can trim it close.

2. To begin, bring the thread through and under the first loop. Leave a thread loop on the outside of the metal loop and sew back under the metal loop and the thread tail.

Sew over the thread tail and the metal loop and go through and under the thread loop.

Figure 1

3. Leave another loop on the outside of the metal loop. Sew under the metal loop to the inside and under then over the thread tail. Bring the needle over the thread tail and the metal loop and down through the new thread loop (figure 1).

Tighten the tail and loops now, and from now on tighten each stitch as you complete it.

4. Repeat this stitch to cover the outer edge of the first loop.

5. To begin covering the next loop, bring the needle up inside the loop, come over it and go down through the thread loop between the metal loops.

6. After covering the last loop, sew under 5-6 stitches to anchor the thread before clipping it.

Starting the Bead Row

1. Anchor single thread securely under the buttonhole stitches at the right-hand loop. Take a tiny back stitch and go under the button hole stitches again, coming out on the edge at the center of the right-hand loop.

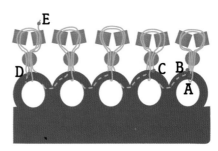

Figure 2

2. String 1 Czech bead and 2 dark bronze Delicas. Sew back into the Czech bead and go through the clasp loop. Reinforce the stitch by repeating the thread path (figure 2, a-b).

3. Sew under buttonhole stitches to the middle of the second clasp loop (figure 2, b-c) and repeat step 2.

Repeat this step for all 5 clasp loops.

4. After anchoring the fifth starting stitch in the buttonhole stitches, sew back out the Czech bead and the next-to-last Delica, the 9th (figure 2, d-e).

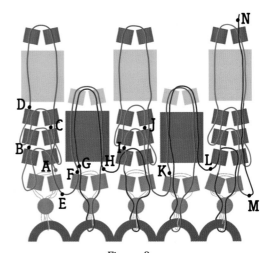

Figure 3

Starting the Herringbone

1a. Pick up 2MC. Sew into the 10th Bronze Delica toward the Czech bead. Then go up the second MC (figure 3, a-b).

b. Pick up 2MC and sew down the first MC of the previous row then up the 2nd MC of this row (figure 3, b-c).

c. Pick up 2MC. Sew down the first MC of the previous row then up the 2nd MC of this row (figure 3, c-d).

d. Pick up 1A Tila (bright bronze) and 2MC. Sew down the other hole of the Tila and 4 beads below it (figure 3, d-e).   e. Then sew up the next bronze Delica (figure 3, e-f).

2a. Pick up 1B Tila (matte bronze) and 2AC.

Sew down the other hole of the Tila and the bronze Delica below it.

Sew down into the Czech bead, go through the clasp loop, and sew back up the Czech bead and the 3rd bronze from the left (figure 3, f-g).

b. Repeat the thread path through the Tila, 2AC, and Tila (figure 3, g-h).

3a. Pick up 2MC and sew down the 6th bronze Delica from the left, into the Czech bead, through the clasp loop, out the Czech bead, through the 5th bronze Delica from the left and then the first new MC (figure 3, h-i).

Work the stitch a little loosely so the beads will line up correctly.

b. Pick up 2MC and sew down the 2nd MC of the previous row then up the 2nd of this row (figure 3, i-j).

c. Pick up 2MC, sew down the first of the previous row and up the 2nd of this row.

d. Pick up 1A and 2MC. Sew down the other hole of the Tila and through the 4 beads below it.*

e. Then sew up the next bronze Delica to the right (figure 3, j-k).

4. Repeat steps 2 (figure 3, k-l) and 3 (figure 3, l-m) to the *. Sew up the 3 outside MC, the outside hole on the Tila and the edge MC (figure 3, m-n).

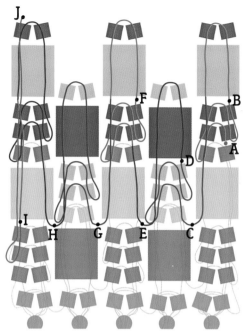

Figure 4

Working the Bracelet Body

From now on, work as follows:

1a. Pick up 2MC and sew down the 2nd MC on the row below then up the 2nd on this row. Pick up 2MC, sew down the first on the row below and up the 2nd on this row (figure 4, a-b).

b. Pick up 1A and 2MC. Sew down the other (inner) hole of the Tila and the 4 beads below it (figure 4, b-c).

2a. Sew up the first AC. Pick up 2AC, sew down the 2nd AC on the row below and up the 2nd of this row.

Pick up 2AC, sew down the first on the row below and up the 2nd of this row (figure 4, c-d).

b. Pick up 1B and 2AC. Sew down the other hole of the Tila and 3AC below it (figure 4, d-e).

3a. Sew up the near hole of the next A and the MC above it.

Pick up 2MC, sew down the 2nd MC on the row below, and up the 2nd on this row. Pick up 2MC, sew down the first on the row below, and up the second on this row (figure 4, e-f).

b. Pick up 1A and 2MC. Sew down the other hole of the Tila and 4 beads below it (figure 4, f-g).

4. Repeat step 2 (figure 4, g-h) then step 3 (figure 4, h-i).

5. To turn so you can begin the next row group, continue down 2 beads below the next-to-top left-hand edge A Tila then go up the 1 below it and the remaining edge beads (figure 4, i-j).

6. Working left-to right, join the new B Tilas to the Delica beads next to them without adding new beads as follows:

Herringbone Bracelet

continued from page 17

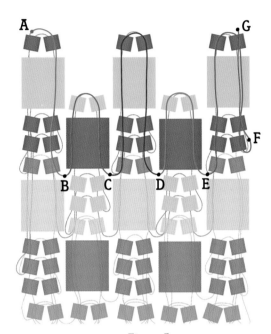

Figure 5

a. Sew down the 2nd MC from the left-hand edge and continue down the inner hole of the A and the 3MC below it (figure 5, a-b).

b. Sew up the new left-hand B, through the 2AC above it, and down the Tila's right-hand hole (figure 5, b-c).

c. Sew up the 3MC beads below the left-hand hole of the middle A and the Tila's hole; then go through the 2MC beads above it and continue down the Tila and the 3MC beads below its right-hand hole (figure 5, c-d).

d. Go up the next B, through the 2AC above it, and down the right-hand hole of the Tila (figure 5, d-e).

e. Go up the next 3MC beads, the A's hole above them, and continue through the 2MC above the Tila. Continue down the Tila and the 2MC below it (figure 5, e-f).

f. Turn by going up the right-hand MC below the edge Tila, the edge Tila, and the right-hand MC above it (figure 5, f-g).

7. Repeat steps 1-5 for the next (3rd) row group and turn on the left-hand edge as before. Repeat step 6 to join the new B Tilas to the adjacent Delica beads.

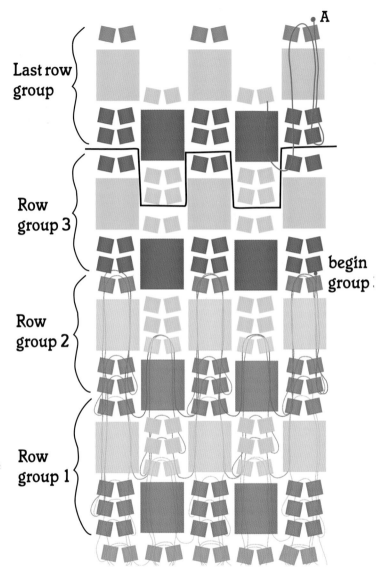

Figure 6

8. Repeat step 7 until the bracelet is about ½" (1.3cm) shorter than desired.

Important: On the last row that you add Delicas, put bronze Delicas above the A Tilas.

Repeat step 6 to join the new B Tilas to the adjacent Delicas.

End with step 6 (figure 6, a).

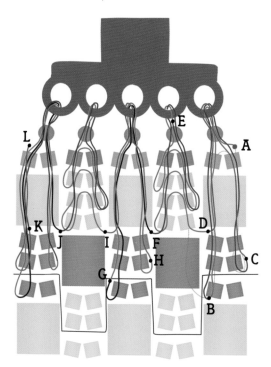

Figure 7

finishing

1a. With the needle coming out the right-hand bronze Delica above the edge A Tila (figure 7, a), pick up a Czech bead and go through the edge clasp hole.

Make sure the second clasp part is correctly aligned with the first.

Go down the Czech bead, the 2nd bronze Delica, the inner hole of the Tila and the 3MC below it (figure 7, a-b, light blue).

b. Reinforce the join by sewing up 2MC, the inner hole of the A, the 2nd bronze Delica, and the Czech bead. Go through the clasp loop again, down the Czech bead, the edge bronze Delica, the edge hole of the Tila, and 2MC below it (figure 7, b-c, blue).

c. Repeat the thread path up the MC below the Tila, the Tila, the first bronze Delica, the Czech bead, and the loop. Then go down the Czech bead, the 2nd bronze, and the inner edge hole of the Tila (figure 7, c-d, red).

2a. Sew up the adjacent AC and add 2 pairs of AC above it as usual. Add a pair of bronze Delicas above

the ACs. String a Czech bead and go through the next clasp loop l (figure 7, d-e, light blue).

b. Go down the Czech bead, the first bronze Delica and 2 AC below it.

c. Reinforce by sewing up the top right-hand AC, the bronze Delica, and the Czech bead. Go through the loop again then down the Czech bead, the 2nd bronze, and the 3AC below it (figure 7, e-f, blue).

3. Sew up the right-hand side of the middle A and the first bronze. String a Czech bead and go through the middle clasp loop. Go down the Czech bead, the 2nd bronze, the left-hand hole of the Tila, and the 3MC below it (figure 7, f-g, dark blue).

Turn and sew up 2MC, the Tila, and the 6th bronze. Go through the Czech bead and the clasp loop. Then sew down the Czech bead, the 5th bronze, the Tila, and 2MC below it (figure 7, g-h, light blue).

Turn and sew up the top right-hand MC, the Tila, the 5th bronze, the Czech bead, and the clasp loop. Sew down the Czech bead, the 6th bronze, and the Tila (figure 6, h-i, red).

4. Repeat step 2 (figure 7, i-j, light and medium blue) then step 3, joining the 9th and 10th bronze Delicas to the last clasp loop.

After going down the Tila the 2nd time (figure 7, j-k, dark, light, and medium blue), continue down the next 2MC Go up the top MC, the Tila , and the left-hand bronze (figure 7, k-l, red).

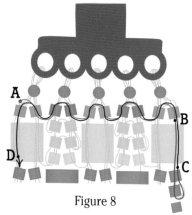

Figure 8

5. To complete the herringbone structure, sew down the 9th bronze, up the 8th, down the 7th, up the 6th, and so forth. End by going down the first bronze (figure 8, a-b).

Reinforce the last row by continuing down the edge of the Tila and 2MC below it. Turn, coming up the top MC (figure 8, b-c), the Tila, and the bronze above it.

Follow the same thread path back through the bronze beads.

End the thread in the left-hand column of beads (figure 8, c-d) with a few pairs of half-hitches (see "Knots") between beads.

SIZE: Pillow Bead: 1" x 1"

Materials

Tila beads:

      10 white (WT),
      10 trans. pink (PT),
      10 metallic green (GT),
      10 luster silver-gray (ST)

1-2g Seed beads, size 11/0, trans. gray
Beading needles, #12
Transparent thread or pale gray K-O beading thread
1 Clear plastic faceted, plump square bead, 20mm
1 Key chain split ring with 3-4 hooks and a swivel
1 Fancy bead, 10-12mm
1 Head pin, silver tone, 2" (5cm)
2 Jump rings, heavy gauge, 8mm
Heavy cable chain, approx. 6 links

Pillow Bead Key Chain

Use a multi-pass version of peyote stitch to weave then trim a Tila bead covering over a clear plastic, square bead. Attach it to a key ring with chain and a jump ring and add hooks, a swivel, and a smaller decorative bead as desired.

How-to

Four Tila beads lie horizontally along the bottom of the bead covering and three along the top. The beads that cover the front, back, and side edges lie vertically.

You add the trim seed beads between the pairs of holes on the Tila beads last.

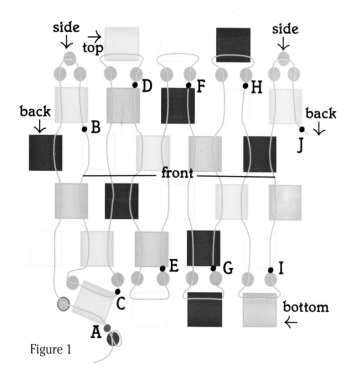

Figure 1

Front Side, Top, and Bottom

The first vertical row adds the beads on the edge of the left-hand back side of the bead as well as the left-hand edge beads.

1. String a stop bead about 6" (15cm) from the end of a 2 yd. (1.8m) thread.

2. Pick up a PT, a seed (outlined in figure 1 – the last seed you go through to finish the back side), a WT, an ST, a GT, and a PT. End with 3 seeds. Sew down the other hole of the PT (figure 1, a-b).

3. Pick up a WT and go through the second hole of the ST. Pick up a PT and a seed and sew through the second hole of the first PT added (on the bottom edge) toward the stop bead (figure 1, b-c).

4. Pick up a seed and go through the second hole of the last PT added in step 3. Pick up a GT and go through the second hole of the WT added in step 3. Pick up an ST, a seed, and a PT (the first top edge bead). End with a seed (figure 1, c-d).

5. Go through the second hole of the ST added in step 4. Pick up a PT and go through the second

hole of the GT. Pick up an ST, a seed, a WT (bottom edge), and a seed (figure 1, d-e).

6. Go through the second hole of the ST added in step 5. Pick up a WT and go through the second hole of the PT. Pick up a GT, a seed, a WT (top edge), and a seed (figure 1, e-f).

7. Go through the second hole of the GT just added. Pick up an ST and go through the second hole of the WT. Pick up a GT, a seed, a GT (bottom edge), and a seed (figure 1, f-g).

8. Go through the second hole of the side GT. Pick up a PT and go through the second hole of the ST. Pick up a WT, a seed, a GT (top edge), and a seed (figure 1, g-h).

9. Go through the second hole of the WT. Pick up a GT and go through the second hole of the PT. Pick up a WT, a seed, an ST (bottom edge), and a seed (figure 1, h-i).

10. Go through the second hole of the WT. For the right-hand side edge. Pick up an ST and go through the second hole of the GT. Pick up a PT and 3 seeds and go down the second hole of the PT (figure 1, i-j).

Pillow Bead Key Chain

continued from page 21

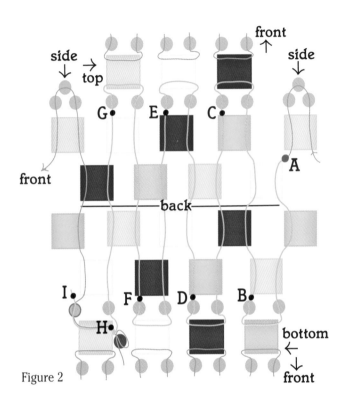

Figure 2

Back Side and Bead Insertion

1. Turn the beadwork over and pick up a WT. Go through the second hole of the side ST. Pick up a PT and a seed and go through the second hole of the bottom ST toward the starting edge of the beadwork. Pick up a seed (figure 2, a-b).

2. Go up through the second hole of the PT, pick up a GT, and go through the second hole of the WT.

    Pick up an ST and a seed. Sew through the second hole of the top GT and pick up a seed (figure 2, b-c).

3. Slip the plastic bead into the forming pocket. It will fit tightly.

4. Go through the second hole of the ST, pick up a PT, and go through the second hole of the GT. Pick up an ST and a seed and go through the second hole of the bottom GT. Pick up a seed (figure 2, c-d).

5. Go through the second hole of the ST. Pick up a WT, go through the second hole of the PT. Pick up a GT and a seed and go through the second hole of the top WT. Pick up a seed (figure 2, d-e).

6. Go down through the second hole of the GT, pick up an ST, go through the second hole of the WT, and pick up a GT and a seed. Go through the second hole of the bottom WT and pick up a seed (figure 2, e-f).

7. Go up the second hole of the GT, pick up a PT, go through the second hole of the ST, and pick up a WT and a seed. Go through the second hole of the top PT and pick up a seed (figure 2, f-g).

8. This row joins the previous back row to the first back row, added at the beginning of the front section.

    Go down through the second hole of the WT added in step 9. Go through the second hole of the GT added at the beginning of the front. Go through the second hole of the PT added in step 7 and then through the second hole of the WT added at the beginning of the front.

    Pick up a seed. Remove the stop bead and tie the starting tail and working thread together securely (figure 2, g-h) Use a surgeon's knot (see "Knots").

    Go through the hole where the stop bead attached to the starting PT (bottom). Continue through the first seed added (figure 2, h-i).

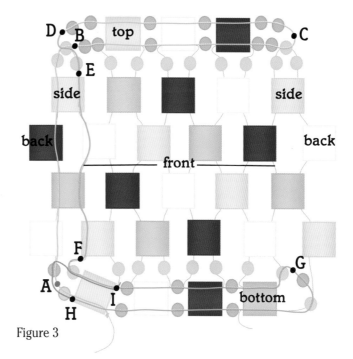

Figure 3

Corners, Top, and Bottom Bead Trim

1. With the needle exiting the first seed strung, pick up a seed. Follow the thread path through the Tilas added on the first row: WT, ST, GT, and PT.

2. Go through the first 2 of the 3 seeds added on the top corner (figure 3, a-b). Pick up 2 seeds and go through the top front edge PT.

Pick up a seed and go through the top front edge WT. Pick up a seed and go through the top front edge GT. Pick up 2 seeds and go through the middle seed of the 3 seed group on the corner (figure 3, b-c).

3. Pick up 2 seeds and, working back toward the start, go through the back hole on the top GT.

Pick up a seed and go through the back hole of the top WT. Pick up a seed and go through the back hole on the top PT. Pick up 2 seeds (figure 3, c-d).

4. Sew through the center bead of the 3-seed group on the first corner toward the front side beads. Go down the other seed of the 3-seed group

Sew through the center bead of the 3-seed group (figure 3, d-e) and follow the thread through the PT, WT, ST, and PT (figure 3, e-f).

5. Go through the seed on the front side edge of the bottom PT and the front hole of the PT.

Pick up a seed and go through the front hole of the WT. Pick up a seed and go through the GT. Pick up a seed and go through the ST and the adjacent seed towart the WT (figure 3, f-g).

6. Pick up a seed and sew through the seed connected to the back hole on the bottom ST.

Go through the back hole of the bottom ST, pick up a seed, go through the back hole on the GT, pick up a seed, go through the back hole of the WT, pick up a seed, and go through the back hole on the PT (figure 3, g-h).

7. Continue through the adjacent seed and the first seed added in step 1.

Go back through the seed adjacent to the front hole of the bottom PT and the PT toward the other end of the bottom (figure 3, h-i).

Pillow Bead Key Chain

continued from page 23

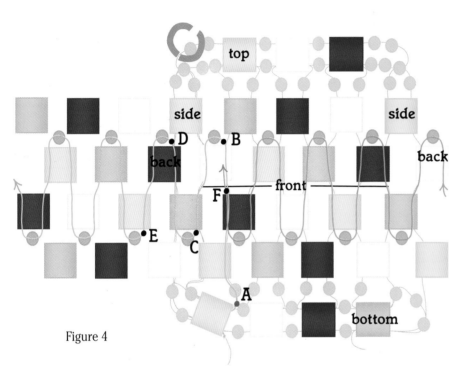

Figure 4

Side Bead Trim

1. Sew through the seed with its hole aligned vertically between the 2 PTs. Sew up through the side PT, the GT, and the WT (figure 4, a-b). Pick up a seed and sew down the other hole of the WT and the ST below and to its left (figure 4, b-c).

2. Pick up a seed and sew up the other hole of the ST and through the GT above and to its left (figure 4, c-d).

3. Pick up 1 seed and sew down the other hole of the GT and through the PT (figure 4, d-e).

4. Repeat this process all the way around the center pairs of Tilas. End by picking up a seed and sewing down the last PT and the GT below and to its left. Pick up a seed and sew up the other hole of the GT (figure 4, e-f). End the thread in the beadwork with several pairs of half hitches between beads (see "Knots").

Repeat with the starting tail.

Assembly

1. Open a large jump ring and pass it through one of the 5-seed corners on the top edge (figure 4, top center).

Insert an end link of the chain into the jump ring and pass the other end through the key chain ring. Then insert it into the jump ring.

Use two pairs of chainnose pliers to close the jump ring tightly (detail photo).

2. For the trim bead, pass the head pin through its hole. Then bend the wire over in a right angle against the top of the bead.

Grasp the wire at the bend with roundnose pliers and pull the tail around a jaw to form two full wraps, turning the pliers in the loop as needed.

Trim the excess wire off at the base of the double loop. Open the other large jump ring and put it on the key ring and through the double loop. Then close the jump ring tightly.

Long Beaded Necklace

Try an elegant combination of lightweight plastic beads, chain, Tila beads,
seed and glass beads for an eye-catching fashion. This necklace is nearly 40 in.
(1 meter) long, which allows you to wear it many different ways.

Long Beaded Necklace

continued from page 25

SIZE: 40"

Materials

78 Tila beads, dark gold metallic AB

25 Tila beads, blue/gold matte metallic

1 Plastic long melon bead, clear and silver, 20 x 13mm

2 Clear faceted plastic pillow squares, 20mm

1 Plastic twisted flat round, milky white, 24mm

1 Plastic round, white pearl, 14mm

2 Textured rings, gold-tone, Tierra Cast pewter, 19mm outside diameter (OD) x 14mm inside diam. (ID)

1 Textured square toggle clasp, gold-tone, Tierra Cast pewter 23mm

9 Oval jump rings, gold-tone, 3 x 4mm

8 Clam-shell bead tips, gold-tone

26" (66cm) Cable chain, gold-tone, 2 x 2.9mm links

12 Eye pins, bronze-tone, 2" (5cm)

5 Eye pins, gold-tone, 2" (5cm)

50 Czech faceted, pressed-glass beads, light sapphire, 4mm

1g Seed beads size 15/0, dark bronze

2g Delica beads, size 11/0, black-lined blue AB

2g Delica cut beads, size 11/0, black-lined amber AB

80 Bugle beads, bronze, 6-6.5mm

4-8 Beading needles, size 12

Beading thread, K-O blue

G-S Hypo Cement or clear nail polish

Round and chainnose beading pliers, diagonal wire cutters

How-to

Assemble the bead and Tila units from the ring end of the clasp to the four oval jump rings. Next assemble the toggle bar, chain, and ring end of the necklace.

Then string the bead strand portion of the necklace with clam-shell bead tips at each end and attach them to the jump rings at each of the first two necklace sections. Be sure to close the jump rings and loops on the eye pins and bead tips tightly.

 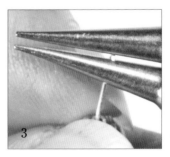

Bead and Tila End (photo 1)

1. String a gold-tone eye pin through each of the plastic beads. Trim the excess wire to $\frac{3}{8}$ " (10mm) and make a matching loop in this end firmly against the bead.

a. To make a wire loop, bend the wire snugly against the bead to a right angle. Grasp the very tip of the wire between the jaws of roundnose pliers at about the 2-2.5mm diameter of the pliers' jaws (photo 2).

b. Press your thumbnail against the right angle bend and your index fingernail into the bend and roll the pliers to form a loop while pressing the pliers gently down toward your nails (photo 3).

If you pull up on the pliers as you roll, the loop will be malformed. Reposition the pliers in the forming loop as needed (photo 4).

c. To open and close loops, shift the cut end of the wire up or down out of the plane of the loop then back into the plane (photo 5). Never pull it outward because this will eventually cause the wire to break.

2. Use two pairs of pliers to adjust the two loops on the bead ends so they are in the same plane.

3. Cut 24 pieces of chain 6 links long (about $^7/16$" / 11mm).

4. Open one loop on each of the 2 square pillow beads, the round pearl, and the melon and catch the end link of 4 chain pieces into each of the loops.

　Close them tightly.

5. Join the free loops on the round pearl and the melon bead to make a 2-bead unit with 4 chains on each end.

6. Attach 4 chain pieces to each of the loops on the flat round.

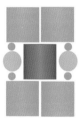

Figure 1

7. Next make 3 Tila units with 4 bronze eye pins each as follows:

　a. String a pin through a hole on a gold Tila, then string a 15/0 seed, a pressed-glass bead, a 15/0, and another gold Tila. Trim the wire as described in step 1 and make a matching loop against the Tila in the same plane as the first loop.

　b. String another eye pin through the other hole of the first Tila. Then string a matte Tila and go through the second hole of the second gold Tila. Complete the pin with a loop as before.

　c. With the third eye pin, string a gold Tila, go through the other hole of the Matte Tila and string another gold Tila. Complete this pin's second loop.

　d. String the fourth pin through the second hole of one of the new gold Tilas, string a 15/0, a pressed-glass bead, and a 15/0. Then go through the second hole on the other new gold Tila and complete the loop (figure 1).

8. As you attach the chain ends to the Tila units, make sure to keep them in order so they hang straight, untwisted, and uncrossed as follows:

　a. Attach the loops at one end of a Tila unit to the chains on the top pillow bead. Join the loops on the other end of this Tila unit to the chains on one end of the flat round bead.

　b. Join the loops on one end of the second Tila unit to the chains on the other end of the flat round bead. Join the loops on the other end of this Tila unit to the chains coming off the round pearl.

　c. Join the chains from the melon bead to the loops on the top of the third Tila unit. Attach the chains on the second pillow bead to the loops on the bottom of the third Tila unit.

9. Cut an 11-link piece of chain (approx. $^5/8$" /16mm). Keeping it untwisted, attach one end to the free loop on the top pillow bead. Pass the end of the chain through the stringing hole on the ring end of the toggle clasp.

　Then attach the end link of the chain to the loop on the pillow bead. Close it tightly.

10. Cut a 12-link piece of chain (approx. $^3/4$" /19mm). Attach one end to the free loop on the other pillow bead. Pass the chain through one of the textured gold-tone rings and attach the end to the same loop on the pillow bead, closing it tightly.

11. To finish this section of the necklace, cut 4 chain pieces each 17 links long (approx. 1 $^1/8$" / 28-29mm). Open 4 of the oval jump rings.

　One at a time pass a chain piece through the texture ring at the bottom of this section and join its ends with a jump ring, closing it tightly.

Toggle Bar End

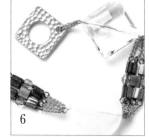

1. Cut a 12-link piece of chain (approx. $^3/4$" / 19mm) and open a jump ring. Pass the chain piece through the second textured ring. Attach the jump ring to the loop on the clasp bar and the two ends of the chain piece (photo 6).

　Close it tightly.

2. Repeat step 11 above to attach 4 chain loops to the other end of the textured ring.

continued from page 27

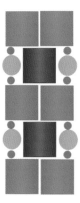

Figure 2

Bead Strand Section

String the 4 bead strands on about 66" (1.7m) of thread doubled. Strand #1 is on the left and strand #4 on the right.

1. To begin, cut a 66" (1.7m) length of beading thread and thread 1 end into a needle. String a 15/0 seed bead to the center then thread the other end of the thread in the same needle. (If this is too difficult, string each end on its own needle).

2. Center the bead on the thread and pass the needle(s) through the bead tip from the inside to the outside so the bead is between the halves of the clamshell and the thread ends are the same length.

3. Repeat steps 1-2 with 3 more clam-shell bead tips.

Press the two halves of each clamshell together to close the bead tips and roll the handle into a neat round loop. (Hint: for best security, roll the handle into a loop before closing the clam shell with the tip of the handle just below the top of the shell.

Put a drop of glue into the shell and close it with pliers so that the tip of the handle is inside the shell. Hold the pliers in place for a minute or two until the glue has begun to set – photos 7 & 8.)

4. Lay the strands on a table in order. Starting at the end that will be attached to the bottom pillow bead, string 5 bugle beads on strands #1 and #4.

String the same length of blue Delicas (about 23) on strand #2 and cut Delicas on strand #3. Adjust the Delica strands to match the length of the bugle strands.

5. For the first Tila group:

a. String strands #1 and #2 through the 2 holes of a gold Tila. On strand #1, string a pressed-glass group (PG) of a 15/0, a pressed-glass bead, and a 15/0, a gold Tila, a PG, and a gold Tila.

b. On strand #2, string a matte Tila, go through the other hole of the second gold Tila, string a matte Tila, and go through the other hole of the third gold Tila.

c. On strand #3, string a new gold Tila, go through the other hole of the matte Tila, string a new gold Tila, go through the other hole of the second matte Tila, and string a final gold Tila.

d. With strand #4, go through the second hole of the first new gold Tila, string a PG, go through the second hole of the middle gold Tila, string PG, and go through the second hole of the last new gold Tila (figure 2).

6. String the same length of cut Delicas on strands #1 and 4, 5 bugles on strand #2, and blue Delicas on strand #3.

Repeat step 5 to make the second Tila group.

7. String blue Delicas on strands #1 and 4, cuts on #2 and Bugles on #3. Make the third Tila group.

8. Repeat steps 4-7 three more times, but do not make a Tila group at the end of step 7.

9. Sew each strand into a bead tip so the needle heads toward the hook. If using 1 needle per strand, unthread one end of each pair and string a 15/0 on the single thread. (If using 2 needles per strand, string the 15/0 on one of the needles.

Tighten the threads to make sure there are no loops or excessive amounts of slack between the two sets of bead tips.

10. Tie the ends of each strand together inside its bead tip over the 15/0 using a pair of surgeon's knots (see "Knots").

Dot the knots with glue then curl the handles and close the new sets of bead tips.

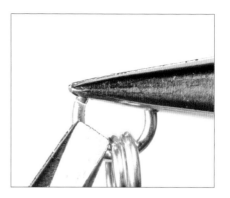

finishing

1. Make sure the chains and jump rings at the pillow bead end of the necklace aren't twisted. One at a time, open the jump rings and attach them to the first set of bead tips.

Close each tightly.

2. Lay out the bead strands so they aren't twisted and the chains and jump rings at the toggle bar end of the necklace the same way.

One at a time open the jump rings and attach them to the bead tips. Close tightly.

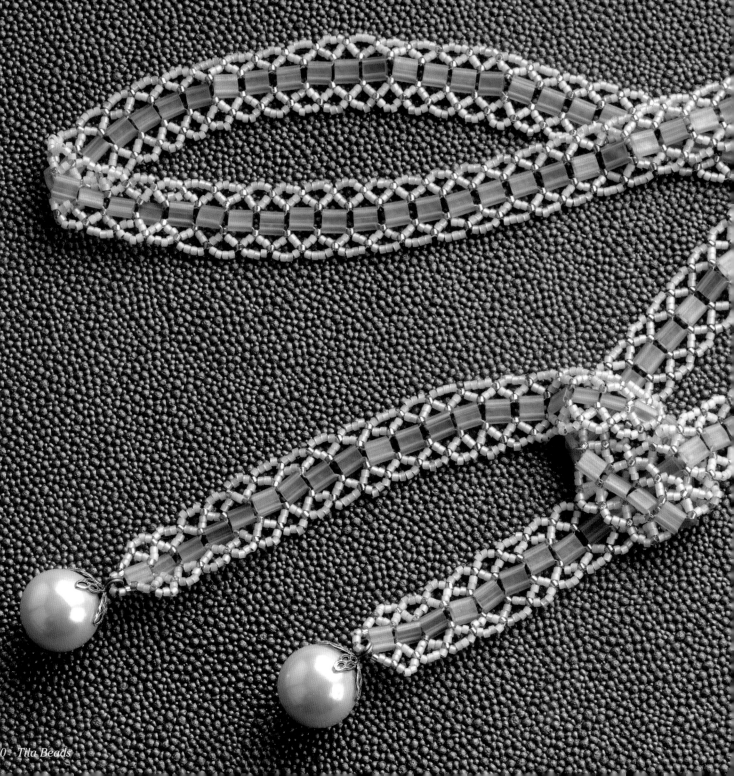

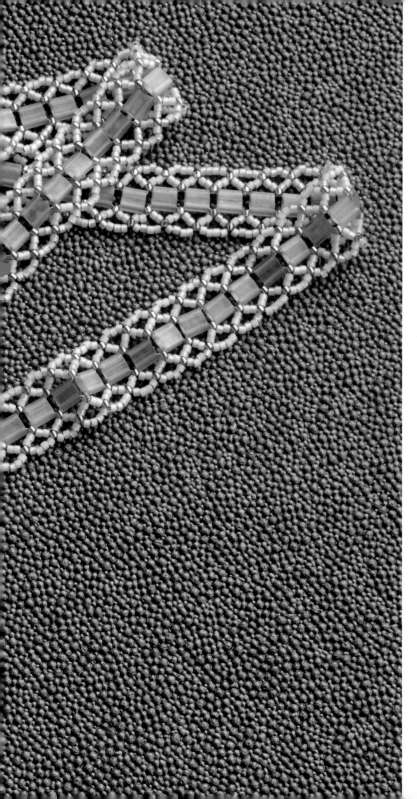

Netted Lariat Necklace

*This gracefully elegant design
is very easy to make and has a
sensational drape.*

SIZE: 36"

Materials

2 Plastic pearls, 16mm
2 Bead caps, silver-tone, petal star, 8-10mm deep
2 Head pins, silver-tone, 1.5 - 2" (3.8-5mm)
5-7g Delica beads, size 11/0, silver-lined milky white (W)
2-3g Delica beads, size 15/0, trans gray silver luster (S)
140 Tila beads, matte sparkle gray (T)
Beading needles, size 12
Beading thread, K-O gray or white

Starting and Adding Thread

1. Work with as long a doubled bead thread as is
comfortable. Too long a thread will tangle easily,
and you will have to add thread no matter how long
your starting thread is.

2. To add thread, stop after adding a Tila (T). With a
new needle and thread, follow the thread path,
starting in the second-to-last T and tying 2-3 pairs of
half hitches around thread between beads as you
work to the point where the short thread exits the
last T.

Continue beading with the new thread. After
several repeats, end the short thread following the
thread path of the new work through the next T and
tying 2-3 pairs of half hitches (see "Knots").

Tila Beads 31

Netted Lariat Necklace

continued from page 31

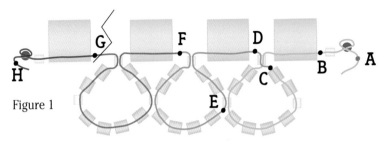

Figure 1

Double-Sided Netting

1. To start, string a stop bead of any color, sewing through it twice without splitting the thread. Leave a 6" (15cm) tail. String a silver 15/0 Delica (S) (figure 1, a-b).

2. String a T, 1S, 2 white Delicas (W), 1S, 4W, 1S, 2W (figure 1, b-c). Sew through the first S after the T toward the T (figure 1, c-d).

3. To work the pattern repeat, String 1T, 1S, and 2W. Sew through S after the first 2W of the previous stitch toward the 4W (figure 1, d-e). String 4W, 1S, and 2W and sew through the first new S toward the new T (figure 1, e-f). Repeat until the lariat is the desired length (figure 1, e-f) — here 140 Tilas or 37" / 94cm — (figure 1, f-g).

4. End with a T and 1S. Then sew on a temporary stop bead, being careful not to split the thread figure 1, g-h). At least 4-6" (10-15cm) of thread must remain. Leave the needle in place.

5. To begin the netting on the other side of the Tilas, start with a new doubled thread and repeat step 1 (figure 2, a-b).

6. To repeat step 2, sew through the other hole on the last T toward the starting end.

7. Continue with the pattern repeat (step 3 — figure 2, b-g). End by sewing out the first T and string 1S (figure 2, g-h).

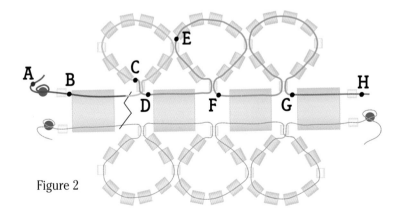

Figure 2

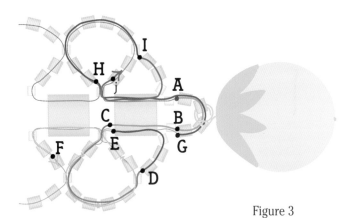

Figure 3

Finishing

1. To finish the starting end, continue working with the second needle. String 4W and sew through the double loop on one of the pearl dangles (figure 3, a-b).

2. Remove the stop bead from the starting thread tail and sew through the first S and the first T toward the final end (figure 3, b-c).

3. Follow the thread path of the first netting loop and sew out the third S (figure 3, c-d). String 2W and 1S. Sew back into the first T (figure 3, d-e).

    End the thread by following the thread path of the first netting loop and tying 2-3 pairs of half hitches between W beads (figure 3, e-f and see "Knots").

    End by going through 2-3 beads. Dot the knots with glue applied from the tip of your needle. Then clip off the excess thread.

4. Thread a needle on the pair of starting tails. Sew through the 4W that attach the pearl, the final S of the second side, the end T, and the S between it and the next T (figure 3, g-h).

    Go through the last net loop, coming out the end S on the loop (figure 3, h-i). String 2W and 1S. Then sew into the end T. End this thread like the other (figure 3, i-j).

5. Finish the other end as in steps 1-4.

Pearl Dangles

1. String a head pin through a pearl and into a bead cap. Wind a double loop tightly against the top of the cap:

    a. Grasp the wire against the bead cap at about the 2mm diam. of your roundnose pliers and begin to pull the wire around one jaw of the pliers. Keep turning the pliers to keep the jaw unobstructed and you pull the wire twice around it (detail photo).

    b. Use diagonal wire cutters to trim the excess wire near the bottom of the loop.

2. Make a second dangle with the other pearl.

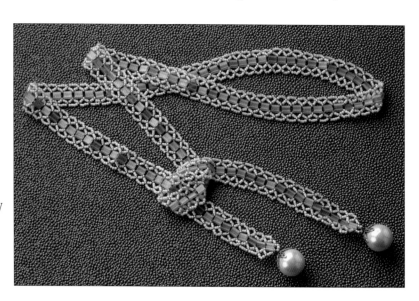

Tila Links Bracelet

This bracelet looks much more complicated than it is, being a simple construction
of woven rings of Tila beads and Delica beads plus three antiqued bronze rings.

SIZE: 6½"

Materials

30 Tila beads, matte metallic blue-green (D)

40 Tila beads, trans. silver-gray AB luster (L)

3-5g Size 10/0 Delicas, trans. topaz black-lined AB luster

3-5g Size 11/0 Delicas, mixed clear dark gold-lined and trans. gray gold-lined

Beading thread, K-O gray

Size 12 beading needles

2 Flat antiqued bronze rings with 2 holes each, 21mm OD (outside diameter) and 14mm ID (inside diameter)

1 Flat antiqued bronze ring with 2 holes, 26.5mm OD and 18.5mm ID

6 Antiqued bronze twist-look jump rings, 7mm

5 Antiqued bronze clover wire charms

1 Antiqued bronze long-and-short chain with 3 large and 4 small links, approx. 27mm

1 Antiqued bronze oval jump ring, 4x5mm

1 Antiqued bronze lobster claw clasp

Starting

1. Use a twist-look jump ring to attach a clover charm to one hole on each small bronze ring and both holes on the large ring. Attach the fifth charm to an end small link on the chain with the oval jump ring.

2. There are two sizes of Tila links: 5 large links made with 8 L (trans. gray) Tilas and size 11/0 Delicas and 5 small links made with 6 D (matte metallic) Tilas and size 10/0 Delicas. Before joining the ends of each link, you pass it through one or more rings and Tila links. Start by making and joining the large links and metal rings.

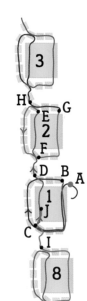

Figure 1

Weaving and Joining the Large Links

1. Use doubled thread to make the large links:

 a. Leaving a 4-6" (10-15cm) tail, pick up an L Tila and 11 size 11/0 Delicas (figure 1, a-b, dark blue). Pass the needle down the same hole on the Tila toward the first Delica and go through the first 3 Delicas (figure 1, b-c, medium blue).

 Go up the other hole on the Tila and sew through the 9th Delica toward the 8th (figure 1, c-d, medium blue).

 b. To begin the next unit of the link, pick up 2 Delicas (the first is a connector bead) and a new Tila (figure 1, d-e, medium blue).

 Pick up 6 more Delicas and sew through the 2nd Delica toward the connector bead (figure 1, e-f, light blue). Pick up 2 more Delicas and sew up the other hole of the Tila (figure 1, f-g, light blue). Pick up 2 Delicas and go through the first of the 6 Delicas toward the 2nd (figure 1, g-h, dark blue).

 c. Make 6 more units as in step b (8 total). With the needle exiting the 3rd Delica at the top of the last unit (figure 1, h-i, medium to light blue), pick up 1 connector Delica.

 Pass the chain through one of the small bronze rings. Make sure the chain lies flat and sew through the 3rd Delica at the bottom of the first unit and up the Tila (figure 1, i-j, red, and figure 2, link 1).

 End the thread with several pairs of half hitches between beads (see "Knots"). Then end the starting tail the same way and trim both.

2. Make another 8-unit chain like the first (steps 1a-b). Pass it through the large metal ring and the large bead link from step 1. Make sure it lies flat and join the ends as before (step 1c figure 2, link 2).

3. Repeat step 1 with the other small metal ring (figure 2, link 3).

4. Repeat step 2 on the other side of the large ring (figure 2, link 4).

5. Make 1 more 8-unit chain. Making sure all the pieces lie flat, pass the new chain through the bead links made in steps 3 and 4 (figure 2, link 5).

 The metal rings are now all linked into a chain with large, light-colored Tila links.

Figure 2

Tila Links Bracelet

continued from page 35

Figure 3

Weaving and Joining the Small Links

Use doubled thread, D Tilas, and size 10/0 Delicas for the small links, which have 6 Tilas each.

1. To make the small links:

a. Leaving a 4-6" (10-15cm) tail, pick up a D Tila and 8 size 10/0 Delicas (figure 3, a-b, yellow). Pass the needle down the same hole of the Tila toward the first Delica and continue through it and the 2nd Delica. Sew up the other hole of the Tila and go through the 7th Delica toward the 6th (figure 3, b-c, orange). Sew down the 6th through 2nd Delicas (figure 3, c-d, dark orange).

b. To begin the next unit, string 3 Delicas (the first is a connector bead) and a Tila. String 6 Delicas (figure 3, d-e, yellow). Sew through the 2nd of the first 3 Delicas toward the third and sew down the other hole of the Tila. Go through the 2nd of the 6 Delicas toward the first (figure 3, e-f, orange).

c. Repeat step b (figure 3, d-f) until you have made 6 Tila units. After completing the 6th unit, string 1 Delica (the joining bead, figure 3, g-h, red).

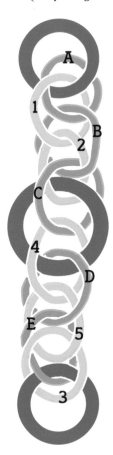

Figure 4

2. Start weaving the small links into the chain at the end with 2 large links. Always make sure everything lies flat before joining the ends of each small link. To complete the first small link, thread it through the first small metal ring and the first large link (figure 4, a).

Pass the needle from the joining bead after the 6th unit through the 7th Delica strung on the first unit toward the 8th and continue through the Tila figure 3, h-i, red) and a few more Delicas, tying pairs of half hitches between beads 2-3 times.

End the starting tail the same way and trim both.

3. Make another 6-Tila dark link. Pass it through the bottom of the first dark link then through the first light link and the 2nd light link before joining its ends (figure 4, b).

4. Make the 3rd dark link and pass it through the 2nd dark link, the 2nd light link, the large metal ring, and the light link that goes through the large ring on the 2nd half of the bracelet (figure 4, c).

5. Join the 4th dark link through the large metal ring and the first and 2nd light rings of the 2nd half (figure 4, d).

6. Join the 5th dark link through the 4th dark link, the middle and end light links and the other small metal ring (figure 4, e).

Finishing

1. Use a large twist-look jump ring to attach the lobster claw clasp to the free hole on one of the small metal rings.

2. Pass the remaining twist-look jump ring through the free small link at the end of the chain and the free hole on the other small metal ring.

Shaped Herringbone Pendant

This pretty pendant combines shaped top and bottom edges with luxurious fringe. This necklace adds an elegance to any formal occasion and stands out boldly against that fabulous little black dress in everyone's wardrobe.

The body alternates 4-Tila bead rows separated by 3 pairs of 3-stacked size 10/0 Delicas with 3-Tila bead rows separated by 4 pairs of 3-stacked size 10/0 Delicas.

Shaped Herringbone Pendant

continued from page 37

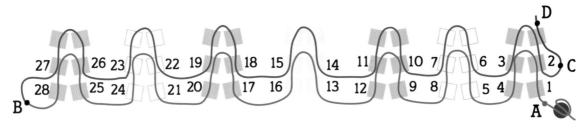

Figure 1

Materials

SIZE: Necklace: 25", Pendant: 1⅜" x 3¾"

5g Delica beads, size 11/0, gold-lined crystal (DG)

1g Delica beads, size 11/0, silver-lined crystal (DS)

5g Delica beads, size 10/0, gold-lined crystal (DMG)

2g Delica beads, size 10/0, white (DMW)

2g Delica beads, size 10/0, clear silk (DMS)

11 Tila beads, clear luster (CT)

9 Tila beads, white (WT)

19 Swarovski bicone crystals, 4mm, white

20 Swarovski bicone crystals, 4mm, crystal

Beading needles, size 12

Beading thread, KO brown

1 Gold-tone metal fob, 6.5-7mm

2 Clamshell bead tips, gold-tone

3 Oval jump rings, 4mm, gold-tone

1 Spring ring, 10mm, gold-tone

3 in. Cable chain, gold-tone, 5mm-long links

True Herringbone Start

1. String a stop bead about 6 in. (15cm) from the end of a comfortably long thread.

2. For the first 2 rows, string 28 size 10/0 Delicas in the following order (see Supplies for color abbreviations):

4DMG, 4DMW, 4DMG, 4DMS, 4DMG, 4DMW, 4DMG.

Figure 1, a-b, numbers the beads and shows how they will be organized when you complete row 3.

3. As you add the beads for row 3 (figure 1, b-c), keep the thread pulled snug and pinch the forming stacks of beads between your thumb and index finger.

Do not split the thread:

a. Sew back through bead #27 toward the start. Pick up 2DMG. Sew through bead #26 toward #25.

b. Skip the next 2 beads and sew through #23 toward the start. Pick up 2DMW and sew through #22 toward #21.

c. Skip 2 beads and sew through #19. Pick up 2DMG and sew through #18.

d. Skip 2 beads and sew through #15. Pick up 2DMS and sew through #14.

e. Skip 2 beads and sew through #11. Pick up 2DMG and sew through #10.

f. Skip 2 beads and sew through #7. Pick up 2DMW and sew through #6.

g. Skip 2 beads and sew through #3. Pick up 2DMG and sew through #2 toward #1. Sew through the second new DMG toward the first (figure 1, c-d).

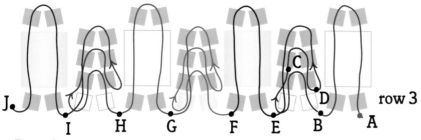

Figure 2

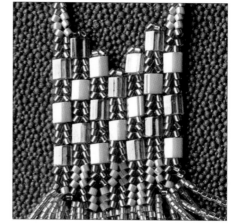

Tila and Triple Gold Rows

1. To begin the first 4-Tila row, working right to left, pick up a WT and 2DMG.

Sew down the second hole of the Tila and the second Delica on row 3 (figure 2, a-b).

2a. Sew up the third Delica and pick up 2DMG. Sew down the fourth Delica.

b. Sew back up the last bead added (figure 2, b-c). Pick up 2DMG and sew down the first bead added in 2a (figure 2, c-d).

c. Sew up the last new bead and pick up 2DMG. Sew down the first bead added in 2b and continue down the 2 new beads below it and the fourth bead on row 3 (figure 2, d-e).

3. Sew up the fifth bead. Repeat step 1 with a CT and 2DMG.

Sew down the second hole of the CT and the sixth bead of row 3 (figure 2, e-f).

4. Sew up the seventh bead of row 3 and repeat steps 2a-c, continuing down the eighth bead of row 3 (figure 2, f-g).

5. Sew up the ninth bead and repeat steps 1 (WT – figure 2, g-h), 2 (figure 2, h-i) and 1 (CT – figure 2, i-j).

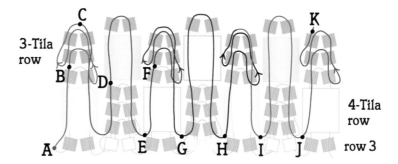

Figure 3

6. To begin the first 3-Tila row, sew back up the last Tila and the DMG above its edge hole (figure 3, a-b).

7. Working left to right, add 2 more pairs of DMG over the end pair as in step 2 (figure 3, b-c). End by going down the 3DMG to the right of the new edge stack and the inner hole of the CT.

8. Then sew up the 3 stacked DMG next to the Tila (figure 3, c-d). Repeat step 1 with a CT and 2DMG. Sew down the second hole of the CT and the stack of 3 Delicas below it (figure 3, d-e).

9. Sew up the near hole of the WT and the Delica above it (figure 3, e-f). Add 2 more pairs of DMG above the pair added on the 4-Tila row and go down the last stack of 3DMG and the inner hole of the WT (figure 3, f-g).

10. Repeat steps 8 (WT – figure 3, g-h), 9 (figure 3, h-i), and 8 (CT – figure 3, i-j). End the row with 2 more pairs of DMG over the right-hand edge pair.

When you have added the third pair of DMG over the WT on the right and turned, your needle will be coming out one stack in from the right-hand edge (figure 3, j-k).

Shaped Herringbone Pendant

continued from page 39

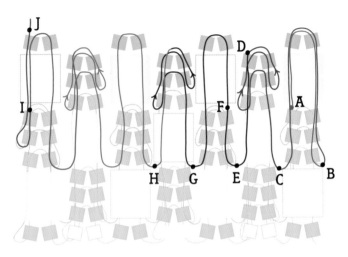

Figure 4

11. To begin the next 4-Tila row (right to left), pick up a CT and 2DMG and go down the other hole of the CT and the 3 DMG on the right-hand edge (figure 4, a-b). Come up the top 2 DMG and the Tila.

Go through the 2DMG above the CT, down the CT, and the 3 DMG one column in from the right-hand edge (figure 4, b-c).

Come up the last Tila of the previous row and the first DMG above it. Work 2 pairs of DMG over the pair of DMG above the Tila (figure 4, c-d). Go down the 3 DMG on the left and the Tila below (figure 4, d-e).

Come up the next column of 3 DMG (figure 4, e-f). *Repeat step 1 with a WT and 2 DMG above it (figure 4, f-g). Repeat step 2 to complete the 3-high pairs of DMG over the middle WT (figure 4, g-h).

Repeat from *, adding a CT and finishing with a WT on the left-hand edge (figure 4, h-i). Go down only 2 DMG on the edge and come up the last DMG of the 3-stack, the WT, and the left-hand DMG (figure 4, i-j).

12. Finish the unshaped portion of the pendant with a 3-Tila row as in steps 6-10, putting a CT in the middle and WTs on each side (figure 5, a-b, dark gray line).

Shaped Top

1. Your needle is exiting one stack to the left of the right-hand edge as in step 10 above. Add a WT and pair of DMG (figure 5, b-c). Then complete a 3-high pair of DMG (figure 5, c-d). Finish the right side with a CT with 2 DMG above it (figure 5, d-e).

2. Go down the CT and the stack of 3DMG below the CT's left-hand hole. Come up the CT in the middle of the 3-Tila row, go through the 2DMG above it then down the left side of the CT.

3. Come up the next stack of 3DMG (figure 5, e-f) and add a WT and pair of DMG. Go down the WT and the 3 DMG below its left-hand hole (figure 5, f-g). Come up the WT on the previous row and the DMG above its right-hand hole.

Complete the 3-high pairs of DMG and go down the left-hand column and the left side of the WT below (figure 5, g-h).

4. Come up the right column of the leftmost set of 3DMG pairs and add a CT and DMG pair above it. End by going down only 2DMG on the left-hand edge (figure 5, h-i).

5. Come up the top DMG, the left-hand hole of the CT, and the DMG above it. Add 2 more pairs of DMG above the first pair (figure 5, i-j). Go down the right side of the 3-bead stack and the CT below it (figure 5, j-k, purple line). Come up the 3 beads to the right and add a

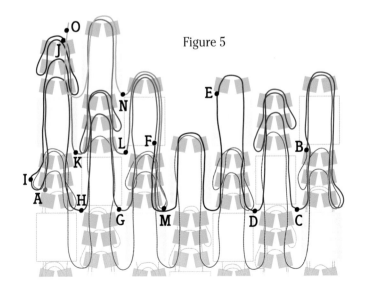

Figure 5

40   *Tila Beads*

CT and pair of DMG.

6. Go down the right side of the new Tila and the 3 beads below it (figure 5, k-l, purple line).

Come up the WT of the 4-Tila row, through the 2 DMG above it, and down the right side of the Tila and the 3 beads below it (figure 5, l-m, dark green line).

7. Turn and come up the 2 beads below the WT. Then go through the right side of the Tila and the 2 beads above it (figure 5, m-n, green line).

Come up the CT to their left, go through the 2 beads above it, down the left-hand side of the CT, then up the 3 beads to its left (figure 5, n-o, light green line).

8. Begin the neck strap on the left side. Coming out the top DMG to the right of the left-hand edge, add 3 pairs of DMW then 3 pairs of DG. Add 3 pairs of DS and 3 pairs of DG (figure 6, a-b). Go down all but the first DMG above the top CT on the left-hand edge (figure 6, b-c).

9. Turn and go up the next DMG. Sew down the 3 DMG to the right of the left-hand edge (figure 6, c-d). Go up the single CT and through the 2 DMG above it.

Go down the Tila and through the 2 DMG above the next Tila (WT on the 4-Tila row – figure 6, d-e). Then go down the WT, through the 2 beads above the center CT, up the third Tila (CT) on the 4-Tila row and through the 2 DMG above it (figure 6, e-f).

10. Go down the Tila and come up the adjacent 3 DMG. Pick up a CT and 2DMG (figure 6, f-g). Sew down the right-hand hole on the new Tila and the 3 DMG below it (figure 6, g-h). Sew up the edge Tila and the first bead above it (figure 6, h-i). Add 2 more DMG pairs (figure 6, i-j).

11. Then complete this side of the neck strap as in step 8, starting to the left of the right-hand edge (figure 6, j). After adding the last pair, sew down the right-hand beads of the neck strap and through the 3 DMG above the edge Tila (figure 6, orange line).

Turn and sew up the next 2 DMG (figure 6, j-k). Then go down the 3 DMG to their left (figure 6, k-l). Sew up the top Tila, through the 2 DMG above it, and down the Tila (figure 6, l-m).

Sew through the 2 DMG above the CT on the last 4-Tila row. Sew down the left side of the Tila and end the thread in the beadwork (figure 6, m-n).

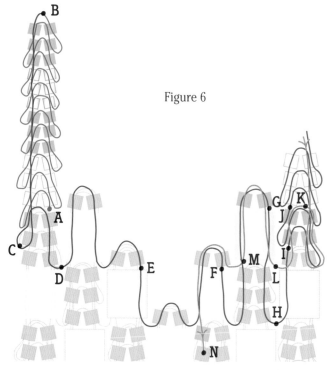

Figure 6

Shaped Herringbone Pendant

continued from page 41

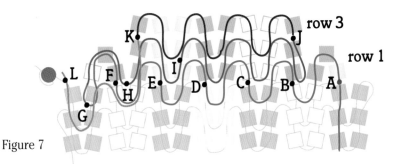

Figure 7

Rounded Bottom Edge

1. Turn the beadwork over so the starting edge is at the top and the stop bead is on the left.

Start a new thread in the second column from the right-hand edge and exit the gold bead (figure 7, a).

2. Pick up a DMS and 2 DMG. Sew into the first DMW from the right then out the second (figure 7, a-b).

3a. Pick up a DMG and a DMW and sew down the fifth bead from the right then out the sixth (figure 7, b-c).

b. Pick up a DMW and a DMG and sew down the seventh bead and out the eighth (both DMS – figure 7, c-d).

c. Pick up a DMG and a DMS and sew down the ninth bead and out the tenth (figure 7, d-e).

d. Pick up a DMS and a DMG and sew down the 11th bead and out the 12th (figure 7, e-f).

e. Pick up 2 DMG and a DMW. Sew down the 13th bead (figure 7, f-g).

f. Turn and sew out the new DMW, through the second DMG, and down the first (figure 7, g-h). Sew up the DMG to its right.

4. For row 2, pick up a DMG and a DMS. Sew down the first silk and out the second (figure 7, h-i).

Add 3 more pairs, maintaining the established color pattern. After going down the right-hand edge DMG, come out the new edge DMG to turn (figure 7, i-j).

5. Add 4 pairs on the third row, maintaining the color pattern (figure 7, j-k).

6. To position your needle for the fringe, after adding the last pair, go down 3 beads. Pull the thread tail through the needle so it is longer than the sewing part of the thread; you are now working with a double thread.

Come up 1, go down 2, and come up 2. The needle exits the first bead strung and points toward the stop bead (figure 7, k-l, orange line).

Fringe

Work the fringe with gold Delicas and alternate white and clear 4mm crystals on the ends, starting and ending with a white crystal.

Groups of 2-3 fringes are joined at their base by brick stitching their first beads together. End and add doubled thread in the herringbone beadwork.

1. For the first fringe string 11 DG, a white crystal, and 5 DG. Sew back down the crystal and the first 11 beads (figure 8, a-b).

2. Pick up the first bead of the second fringe and sew back down the first bead of the first fringe. Tighten so the two beads lie side-by-side and sew out the new bead (figure 8, b-c).

String 12 more DG. End the fringe with a clear crystal and 5 DG and sew back down the crystal and the 13 DG of the fringe (figure 8, c-d).

3. Brick stitch the first bead of the third fringe to the first bead of the second fringe and string 14 more DG (figure 8, d-e). End the fringe as before, remembering to alternate crystal colors.

Anchor the third fringe to the next bead on the bottom edge by sewing down the DMW and the DMG below it (figure 8, e-f). Sew back out the DMW to turn and begin the fourth fringe.

4. Brick stitch the next 3 fringes together: #4 has a base of 16 DG, #5 has 19 and #6 has 20. Anchor the group by sewing left to right through the horizontal DMG (figure 8, g-h).

5. Brick stitch #7 (21 DG) and #8 (23 DG) together. Anchor them by sewing out the first DMG on the third bottom row (figure 8, h-i).

6. Join #9 (24 DG) and #10 (26 DG) together. Sew down the first silk bead and the one below it then out the end silk bead (figure 8, i-j).

7. Brick stitch fringes #11 (28 DG) and #12 (30 DG) together. Sew down the second silk bead and the one below it then out the edge bead (figure 8, j-k).

8. Brick stitch fringes #13 (32 DG) and #14 (34 DG) together. Sew down 2 DMG and out the first (figure 8, k-l).

9. Pick up the first bead for #15 and

brick stitch it to the first bead of #14 (figure 8, l-m). Sew back out #15 and string 34 more DG. Brick stitch #16 (34 DG) to #15. Anchor it by sewing down the next 2 DMG and back out the edge bead (figure 8, m-n).

10. Pick up the first DG for #17 and brick stitch it to #16 (figure 8, n-o). Then string 29 more DG. Anchor it by sewing down 2 DMW and out the end bead (figure 8, o-p).

11. Join #18 (29 DG) and #19 (29 DG) together. Sew down the next 2 DMW and out the end bead (figure 8, p-q).

12. Work #20 (26 DG) and #21 (24 DG) together. Sew into the last DMG of bottom row 3 (figure 8, q-r).

13. Work #22 (24 DG) and #23 (23 DG) together. Sew through the horizontal DMG on the right-hand side (figure 8, r-s).

14. Brick stitch #24 (20 DG), #25 (18 DG), and #26 (15 DG) together. Sew down the silk bead added at the beginning of the bottom shaping and the DMG below it. Sew out the silk (figure 8, s-t).

15. Brick stitch #27 (15 DG), #28 (13 DG), and #29 (11 DG) together. Sew down into the edge DMG of the starting row (figure 8, t-u). Then end the thread in the herringbone.

Remove the stop bead and end the tail in the beadwork.

Necklace

1. Cut a 26 in. (66cm) length of thread and put a needle on each end. Pass one needle through the thread between the last DG herringbone pair on one side of the top (figure 6, b).

Center the thread so the ends are the same length.

2. Hold the needles together and string a DMW, a clear crystal, and a DMW.

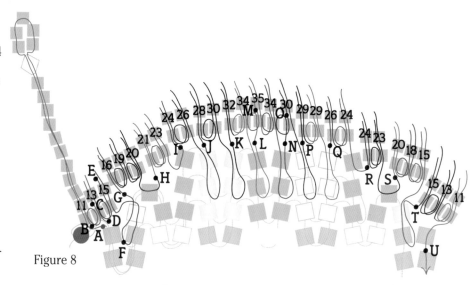

Figure 8

3. On each needle, string 1¾"(4.4cm) of DGs.

4. Hold the needles together and string a DMS, a white crystal, and a DMS.

5. Repeat steps 3, 2, 3, and 4. Then string 3¾" (9.5cm) of DG on each needle. End with another step 2.

6. Pass both needles into the hole of a bead tip. String a DG on one of the needles.

Remove excess slack from both threads then tie them together tightly with 2-3 surgeon's knots inside the bead tip (see "Knots") and dot the knot with glue.

Curl the handle of the bead tip into a secure loop and close the bead tip (see "Long Beaded Necklace," photos 9 & 10).

7. Repeat steps 1-6 on the other side.

8. Attach a fob to one end of the chain piece with a jump ring (see "Long Beaded Necklace," photo 7).

Use another jump ring to attach the other end of the chain to one of the bead tip handles.

9. Join the spring ring clasp to the other bead tip's handle with the third jump ring.

Figures of 8 Tila Necklace

This clever design unites strung side and back sections of figure – eight seed beads around chains of faux pearls. The front is an unusual circularly woven path of Tila beads and picots.

SIZE: 18½"

Materials

14 Plastic pearls, dark gray, 8mm
2 Plastic swirled melon beads, black, 17 x 12mm
20 Jump rings, antique silver-tone, 6mm, heavy gauge (16-gauge)
1 Hook and loop clasp, silver-tone pewter by *Tierra Cast*, swirled fan
2 Clamshell bead tips, antique silver-tone
2 Crimp beads, 1 x 1mm or mini crimps, silver
16 Eye pins, antique silver-tone, 1½" - 2" (3.8-5cm)
38 Tila beads, shiny black (BT)
20 Tila beads, metallic, matte dark gray (GT)
5-7g Seed beads, size 11/0, shiny black (B)
1-2g Seed beads, size 11/0, nickel-plated (N)
2g Triangle seed beads, metallic gray-lined crystal (T)
44 in. (112cm) Flexible beading wire, size .012-.014
Beading needles, size 12
Beading thread, black K-O

How-to

Sides and Back of Necklace

1. String each of the pearls on an eye pin and trim the excess wire to ⅜" (10mm). Make a loop above each pearl, and use pliers to make sure both loops are in the same plane (see "Long Beaded Necklace," p. 26).

2. String a triangle bead, a melon, and a triangle bead on each of the remaining 2 eye pins, and complete loops above the beads as in step 1.

3. Link 7 pearls with 6 jump rings and use another jump ring to link a melon bead to one end of the chain. Attach a jump ring to the free loop above the first pearl and another to the free loop below the melon bead.

Repeat to make a second identical chain.

Figures of 8 Tila Necklace

continued from page 45

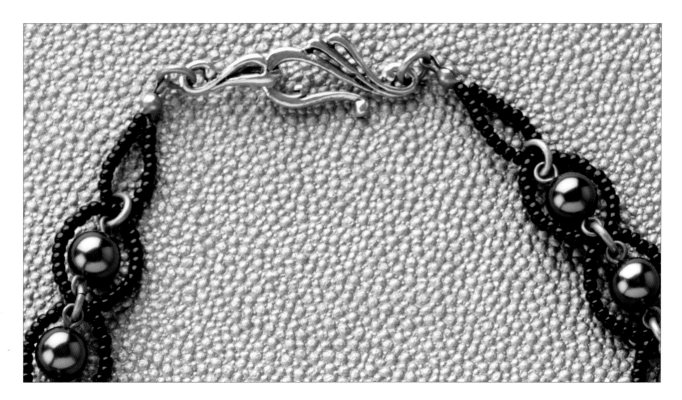

Sides and Back of Necklace

continued

4. Cut the flexible beading wire into 2 pieces, each 22" (55cm) long.

5. See the Supplies list for the bead abbreviations. With one piece of wire, string a BT, GT, and a BT to the center.

String 10B on each end of the wire. Cross the wire tails through another B and the jump ring below a melon bead.

6. String 22B on each end and cross them through another B and the jump ring above the melon bead. Make sure the wire ends are the same length.

7. String 13B on each end and cross them through another B and the next jump ring of the chain.

Repeat this step 6 more times, ending by crossing through another B and the top jump ring.

8. String 10B on each end. Make sure the beads are all pushed snugly together with no slack in the wire.

9. Thread both tails into a bead tip toward the hook and string a crimp bead over them, pushing it snugly against the inside bottom of the bead tip.

Flatten the crimp securely with chainnose pliers and trim off the excess wire.

10. Curl the handle of the bead tip into a loop with roundnose pliers and close the bead tip (see photos 7 & 8 of "Long Beaded Necklace").

Add the Clasp

11. Use a jump ring to attach the loop of the bead tip to that on one of the clasp parts.

12. Repeat steps 5-11. with the other wire and bead chain.

Beadwoven Center

To make the beadwoven center curve, there are fewer edge beads on the top edge, the right-hand side of figures 1-4, than on the bottom edge.

1. Start the beadwork by leaving a 4"-6" (10-15cm) thread tail to weave in later.

a. Sew left to right through the free hole of the right-hand BT. String a B, and sew right to left through the top hole (with the beading wire in it). Continue through the bottom hole of the GT.

b. String a B and go left to right through the top hole of the GT. String 5B and go through the jump ring below a melon bead (figure 1, a-b). Continue left to right through the top hole of the GT.

c. String a B and go right to left through the bottom hole. Repeat the thread path to reinforce the joining of the beadwork to the chain. End going right to left through the top hole of the left-hand BT (figure 1, b-c).

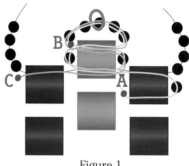

Figure 1

2. In weaving the bead section, note that you put BTs on the edges and GTs in the center. Begin as follows:

a. Pick up 1B and go left to right through the bottom hole of the left-hand BT.

b. String a GT and a B. Go right to left through the other hole of the new GT (center Tila) and string 1B (figure 2, a-b).

c. Circle through the GT and the first B again, exiting the bottom hole to the left. String a BT for the left-hand side (necklace bottom) (figure 2, b-c).

d. Then string 1N, 1B, 1T, 1B, and 1N. Sew left to right through the bottom hole of the previous BT. Continue through the top hole of the new GT and through the bottom hole of the right-hand BT (figure 2, c-d).

e. String 1B, 1T, and 1B then a new BT (figure 2, d-e).

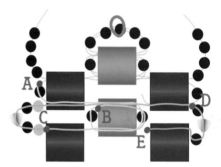

Figure 2

3. Work the pattern repeat as follows:

a. Go right to left through the bottom hole of the last GT and continue through the top hole of the last left-hand BT.

b. String 1B and go left to right through the BT's bottom hole (figure 3, a-b).

c. String a new GT and 1B. Sew right-to left through the bottom hole of the new GT. String 1B and sew left to right through the top hole of the new GT. Continue through the first B and the bottom hole of the GT (figure 3, b-c).

d. String a new BT, 1N, 1B, 1T, 1B, and 1N and go left to right through the bottom hole of the BT above.

e. Continue through the top hole of the newest GT (figure 3, c-d). Sew through the bottom hole of the last right-hand BT. Sew through the edge B toward the T.

f. String 1T, 1B, and 1 BT (figure 3, d-e).

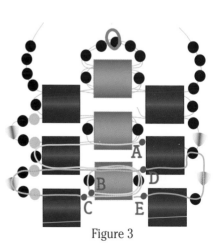

Figure 3

Figures of 8 Tila Necklace

continued from page 47

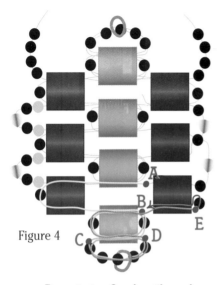

Figure 4

g. Repeat step 3, a-f until you have picked up the 20th GT (figure 4, a-b).

4. To end the beaded section and attach it to the jump ring below the second melon bead:

a. Pick up 1B and sew right to left through the bottom hole of the GT. String 1B and go left to right through the top hole of the GT and the first B.

b. Go right to left through the bottom hole of the GT (figure 4, b-c).

c. String 5B and sew through the jump ring below the melon bead. Continue right to left through the bottom hole of the GT.

d. Repeat the thread path through the 5B (figure 4, c-d) then the GT.

e. Sew through the B on the left-hand side of the GT then through its top hole and the bottom hole on the last right-hand BT (figure 4, d-e).

String 1B and go back through the bottom hole of the same BT. End the thread securely in the beadwork.

Wave Bracelet

This clever design forms a wave shape because you weave the picot edge beads together on one side while leaving them separate on the other and reverse sides every six pattern repeats.

SIZE: 8½"

Materials

3-5g Seed beads, size 11/0, dark bronze (B)
2-3g Seed beads, size 11/0, bright gold (G)
3-5g Seed beads, size 8/0, metallic green
60 Tila beads, matte metallic green (GT)
31 Tila beads, metallic bronze-purple (BT)
Beading thread, K-O, green
Beading needles, size 10 or 12
Hook and loop clasp by *Tierra Cast*,
    bright gold-tone pewter
2 Heavy-weight, jump rings, 6mm, bright gold-tone

Wave Bracelet

continued from page 49

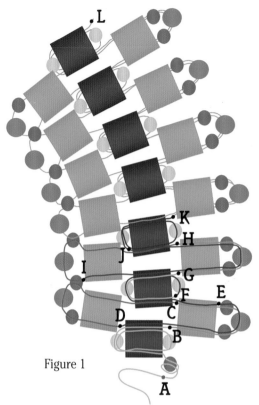

Figure 1

How-to

Work two and one-half pattern repeats for an 8½" (21.3cm) bracelet.

1. Thread a needle with a comfortably long length of thread and work with it single.

Leave a 12" (31cm) tail for adding a clasp part to the starting end and string a temporary stop bead by sewing through it twice without splitting the thread.

2. Start by picking up a BT (bronze-purple Tila) and a G (gold) seed bead. Sew back toward the starting tail through the second hole of the Tila.

Pick up 1G and sew back through the first Tila hole, through the first G and back through the second Tila hole (figure 1, a-b).

First Half Pattern Repeat

1. Pick up a GT, a B, an 8/0, and a B. Sew leftward the second hole of the GT (figure 1, b-c).

2. Pick up a BT, a GT, a B, an 8/0, and a B. Sew back through the second hole of this Tila (figure 1, c-d).

Continue through the second hole of the first BT, the first hole of the first GT, and the 3 seeds above it (figure 1, d-e).

3. Pass the needle leftward through the second hole of the GT and the first hole of the new BT.

4. Pick up 1G and sew back through the second hole of the BT. Pick up 1G (figure 1, e-f) and go back through the first hole of the Tila, the first G, and the second hole of the BT (figure 1, f-g).

5. Pick up a GT, a B, an 8/0, and a B. Sew leftward through the second hole of the GT (figure 1, g-h).

6. Pick up a BT, a GT, a B, and an 8/0. Sew down the near B on the edge of the previous Tila (figure 1, h-i).

7. Sew through the other hole of the new GT, the second hole of the previous BT, the first hole of the first new GT, and the 3 seeds above it.

Continue left through the second hole of this Tila and go through the first hole of the latest BT (figure 1, i-j).

8. Pick up a G and go through the other hole of the BT.

Pick up a G and go down the first hole of the BT, through the first G and back through the second hole of the BT (figure 1, j-k).

9. Repeat steps 5-8 (figure 1, g-k) until you have 6 GT on each edge of the band and end with step 8 (figure 1, l).